Mad About
Mega Beasts!

For James, Pippa and Emma, with love – G.A.

Mega XXXs for Tony – D.W.

ORCHARD BOOKS
338 Euston Road, London NW1 3BH
Orchard Books Australia
Level 17/207 Kent Street, Sydney, NSW 2000

First published in 2014 by Orchard Books
ISBN 978 1 40832 935 1

Text © Giles Andreae 2014
Illustrations © David Wojtowycz 2014

The rights of Giles Andreae to be identified as the author and
David Wojtowycz to be identified as the illustrator of this work
have been asserted by them in accordance with the
Copyright, Designs and Patents Act, 1988.

A CIP catalogue record for this book
is available from the British Library.

1 3 5 7 9 10 8 6 4 2
Printed in China

Orchard Books is division of Hachette Children's Books,
an Hachette UK company.

www.hachette.co.uk

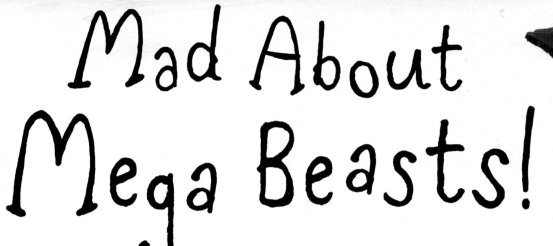

Mad About Mega Beasts!

Giles Andreae

Illustrated by
David Wojtowycz

ORCHARD

Can you spot us in every picture?

Some of us live on the land
And some live in the sea.
Some of us are fierce
And some are gentle as can be.

Some of us like grass and leaves
And other tasty plants.
Some eat up whole animals
Without a second glance!

But one thing that describes us all
By land or sea or air,
Is – we're absolutely MEGA
. . . so meet us if you dare!

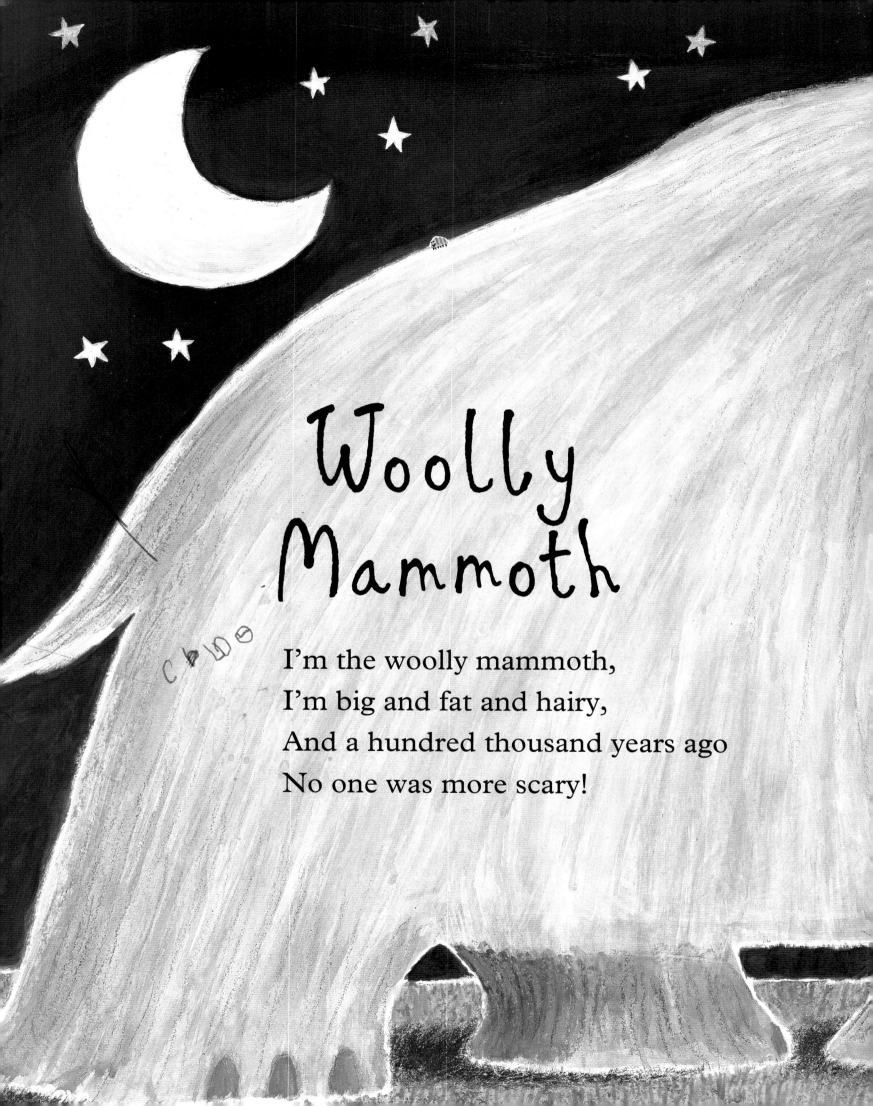

Woolly Mammoth

I'm the woolly mammoth,
I'm big and fat and hairy,
And a hundred thousand years ago
No one was more scary!

Emperor Penguin

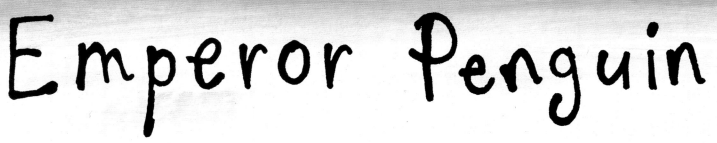

We emperor penguins have got a great trick,
Which makes us chaps feel pretty neat.
While our wives go out hunting
And looking for food,
We hatch out our chicks on our feet!

Elephant Seal

I've got this weird trunk at the end of my nose
But I just have to like it or lump it.
I blow it to frighten my rivals away,
A bit like a giant great trumpet!

Giant Squid

I've got giant eyeballs, eight arms and a beak,
My body weighs almost a ton.
Of all of the creatures down here in the deep,
I must be the weirdest one!

Giant Manta Ray

I glide like a bird through the water
With wings that are silent and free.
Of all other fish in the ocean,
There's not one as graceful as me!

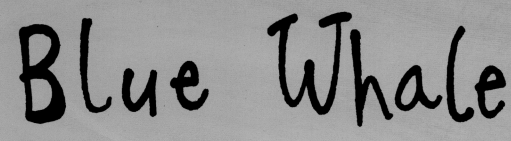

Blue Whale

I'm the largest living mammal
That the planet's ever seen,
Cruising through the ocean
Like a giant submarine!

Argentinosaurus

(Ar-jen-TEEN-oh-sor-us)

I'm the largest dinosaur
The Argentinosaurus.
I'm as big as eighteen elephants
And that is just enormous!

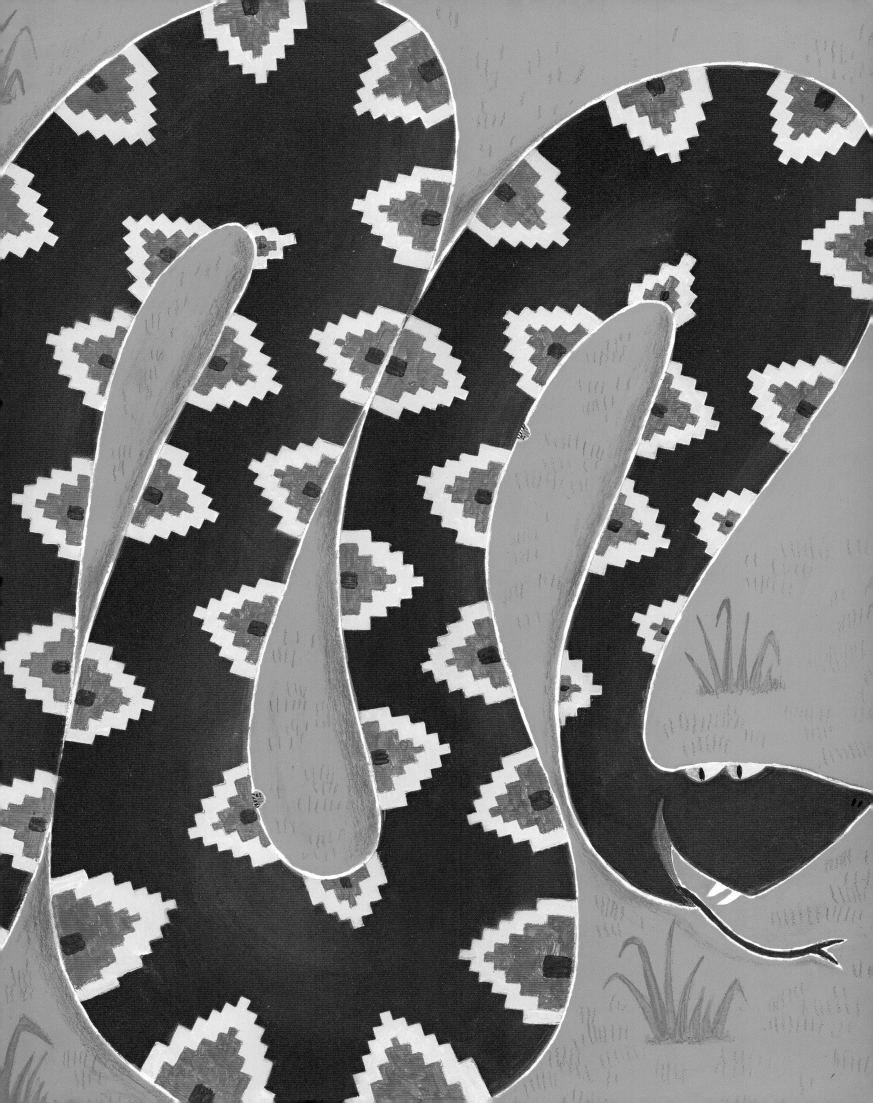

St Bernard

I am the giant St Bernard,
No dog is bigger than me.
My coat is all fluffy
And furry and warm
Why don't you stroke it and see?

Buffalo

A buffalo's horns are all curvy and long
And we don't like to boast as a rule,
But we're also ferocious
And handsome and strong.
Let's face it – we look pretty cool!

Siberian Tiger

I'm the Siberian tiger

The largest big cat in the land,

So don't try to stroke me

Or tickle or poke me

Because I'll just bite off your hand!

Brown Bear

I am the biggest of all of the bears
I weigh just as much as ten men.
But when I feel dozy
I snuggle up cosy
And cuddle my cubs in our den!

So now you've met the mega beasts,
Every single one.
Some are pretty frightening
But some are rather fun!

Some make scary noises
Like a bellow or a roar,
And others you would cuddle
If they came to your front door.

But all of them are pretty huge
I hope you were impressed.
Which one was the scariest
And which did you like best?